WORKING
IN
FLOUR

Books by Jeff Friedman

The Record-Breaking Heat Wave
Scattering the Ashes
Taking Down the Angel
Black Threads
Working in Flour

For Jenny —
fun working in your
office with you —
and thanks for all the
help and the motivation
to utilize the technology —

WORKING
IN
FLOUR

Jeff Friedman (signature)

JEFF FRIEDMAN

December 2011

Carnegie Mellon University Press
Pittsburgh 2011

ACKNOWLEDGMENTS

My thanks to the editors of the following publications in which these poems first appeared:

5 AM: "Walking Uphill: A Memoir," "The War on Fat," "Bridge Street Café," and "Ugliness"
10 x 3 plus: a poetry journal: "Notes from a Love Life" and "Breaking Pitch"
Agni Online: "Notes from the Emperor"
Alehouse: "No One Called" and "Ishmael"
American Poetry Review: "I Did It" and "Yom Kippur"
Ars-Interpres: "Samson Dying" and "Ladder"
Connotation Press: "New Tape of Bin Laden"
Contemporary American Voices: "Left Hand," "Presidential Logic," and "My Shammai"
Cortland Review: "Comice," "Sunday Morning Breakfast," "The Orgasm in Late
                Afternoon," and "Rosh Hashanah"
Dirty Napkin: "Price of a Kiss"
Hampden-Sydney Poetry Review: "Night of the Gnat"
Natural Bridge: "The Binding"
Home Planet News: "Father to Son"
Inertia: "Sotto Voce"
La Petite Zine: "On Behalf of the Prick" and "In My Book"
Literary Imagination: "Rebekah"
Margie: "Poem for Ross Gay," "T.S. Eliot Was a Great Poet," and "Salesman"
Naugatuck River Review: "Route 12"
The New Republic: "Phaeton"
Ontario Review: "Working in Flour"
OVS Magazine: "Shallot" and "Walking with Chuck"
Poetry International: "Son of Apollo"
Pearl: "Learning the Torah"
Prairie Schooner: "Bob Dylan Is God"
River Styx: "Sunday at the Deli"
The 2River View: "Luna Moth" and "The Survivors"
Zeek: "Hagar," "Cashing In," and "Iraq"

My thanks to Colleen Randall, Bekka, Charna Meyers, and Karen Berger for their love
and encouragement. My thanks to Roy Nathanson, Dzvinia Orlowsky, Carol Frost,
Ken Smith, and Steven Schreiner for their help on so many of these poems. I also wish
to thank Howard Schwartz, Alicia Ostriker, and Judith Vollmer for reading and com-
menting on earlier drafts of my manuscript. And my deepest gratitude to my editor,
Gerald Costanzo, for his belief in my poetry.

Book design: Gabriel Routh

Library of Congress Control Number 2010928356
ISBN 978-0-88748-533-6

10 9 8 7 6 5 4 3 2 1

for Colleen and my sister Karen

What can stop us from telling the truth with a laugh

—Horace

Contents

Four

PHAETON

History tells the story
again and again. Horses buck.
A chariot runs wild, reins ripped
from the son's grasp. Missiles fall.
Below, seeds blow through armored bellies.
A rainbow floats south in the tarry ooze.
The mangled armies clash in the dust.
Villages collapse into sinkholes.
Families lie under debris.
The son says a prayer,
rampaging over charred roads.

ONE

I Did It

I took all the free samples
at the chocolate shop
even though the lady
behind the counter frowned
after my first handful
and tried to wrest
the basket from my grip. I walked out
without buying a single chocolate,
though I had sat there for hours
sipping hot water through a straw.
I know what you think: I give Jews
a bad name, even though I'm small
and furry like a nice pet,
except for the hackles
and jagged teeth,
which sometimes wound my lips.
At the diner I asked so many
questions about the dinner specials
the waitress never came back to our table
and I haggled with a spider
over the cost of a fly
for so many hours he dropped
from exhaustion, breaking
into tears. And I demolished
a whole chicken, but didn't
empty the bones
from the plate in the fridge.
I did it: I broke a seal,
stuck the label on the sink,
called you sweetie
when I meant something else.
No, this was not shame
or guilt. It was not
the usual desire to punish. I did it
quick as a passing thought.
The dog couldn't believe
my audacity, and howled
for help. The canary wrote

a letter to our congressman,
complaining about the state
of the union, spitting out seeds
as she spoke. I left the seat up,
a trail of yellow drips,
my piss sweet as a valentine
burning the tiles.

WORKING IN FLOUR

When I walked into the bakery at my usual time
asking politely for two marble cookies,
a fudgy chocolate drop rising from the chocolate swirls,
Ida Kaminsky, who came from strong Russian stock—
a hearty vegetable stew, spicy meats rolled in
cooked cabbage—winked and asked if I wanted a job.
She offered me two bucks an hour,
half off on the marble cookies, and anything
not sold at the end of the day might also be mine.
I put on an apron, pushed through
the swinging doors to help the bakers.
The smell of flour was thick
and tree pollen spotted the windows.
Tall and freckled, Max, the other assistant,
squeezed my hand, "I'll show you what to do."
He taught me how to use the cake decorator,
how to prepare the éclairs and put them in their doilies,
then pointed out the brooms and mops, the industrial
strength cleansers, the double sink
with rubber hoses coiled in it. "You don't want
paste to harden in the bowls."
From across the room, where he scooped chocolate chip
cookie batter onto a baking tray, Julius, the baker,
snapped, "Make sure you tell him: Everything
has to be spick-and-span." The flies heard him
and flew off the lip of the sink toward the light fixtures.
Soon I began sneezing, my hapless ahchoos
running down spotted walls, glistening
on my face and hands as I pumped the custard
through a nozzle into the delicate éclair rolls.
Later, when I worked on cleaning the floors,
Max yelled at me for spreading the dirt
in circles with my mop.
I stepped back, kicking over the bucket of lye.
All in a day's work, I thought.
The next morning, Ida Kaminsky cornered me,
"I liked you better as a customer."
I folded my apron neatly without arguing back

picked up my bag of cookies
and walked out into the bright spring air,
where now I understood my mother's comment,
"You're allergic to work" and where, for a moment,
I stopped sneezing.

POEM FOR ROSS GAY

In the time it took me
to cut four Athena melons
Ross ate them.
Then he ate the entire container
of Mediterranean hummus
on a loaf of organic
sprouted spelt bread.
To distract him from his hunger,
I brought in
Larry Levis's book *Elegy*,
and he said his favorite poem
was the one about the cook
growing lost in his village—
whatever that means.
He flipped through the pages
and read the poem aloud.
"That's a great poem," he said.
He stretched out his long legs
and arms and smiled.
Then he ate the book, too.
But he wouldn't eat
the chocolate chip cookies
or the King Arthur chocolate
onyx wafers because his body
is a temple. Nor would he eat
the balsamic chicken, though
he scrambled all the eggs
over peppers and onions
and polished them off.
"Stay out of the kitchen,"
I ordered, "the fridge is empty."
"Let's do kettle bells," he replied
and pulled out a twenty-five pound
iron ball with a handgrip.
When did you escape
from the chain gang, I asked.
He began swinging it
from between his legs up

over his head faster
and faster until he let it go.
The ball cracked open
the cathedral ceiling,
flying into the sky
like a bomb in reverse.
Tree branches fell.
Glass shattered. The phoebes
cleared out of town quick.
The kettle bell exploded
in a cloud, pieces
of gold nougat and caramel
falling on our table.
Then Ross ate the sun
and pretty soon, he was glowing.

OMEN

From the high branches of the hemlock, a bird
dove through the window, light and dust
falling behind it. Shards shone
on the floor like dice.

Stunned, the bird hunched near the broiler—
red collar, white breast spotted brown,
puffed out, wings tucked—a red-shouldered hawk.
Even when I brought him water, he didn't move.

I opened all the doors and windows,
then came up behind him, listening for his voice—
a yelp of pain, a prophecy bitten
under the beak, a whispered song—

but silence whirled around him, like leaves
caught in a gust of wind. Was he dying
or remembering small birds whose necks he snapped?
Was he gathering himself to attack

or attempt an escape? He spun awake,
hurtling through the open door to the ravine,
red feathers raining over me,
sticking to my hair and shoulders.

Hagar

I was beauty, leading you
down into a secret canal,
your arms rowing toward me.

She was the mirror where you imagined
a kingdom, the treacherous face,
the eyes that claimed you.

I passed through at night, a long kiss, a shiver.
She held you, a locked jaw,
a knock in the ribs, gnashing teeth,

bitter lips, the call to come now,
as jackals circled the fires.
I knelt at a dry well. She knelt at your feet,

urging you to lie down, to try again.
Above, tribes of stars waited.
Dust took my hand, whispered to me.

She was a wound
bleeding into your hands.
My son roamed the desert, aimed

his arrows, killing what he could.
Her son died a thousand times.
She wanted the future. I wanted you.

Summer 1973

Then, my lover hated
herself so much she
attempted to drive a nail
through my forehead. I opened
my eyes in the nick of time
and rolled off the bed while she nailed
the pillow to our mattress.
Lying on the hard floor
I felt the need to pee
as I admired the lovely plumpness
of her breasts. "Did I do something?"
"It's not you," she cried.
That summer was the hottest on record.
Nests frayed in the trees.
Shirts sweat holes in themselves.
Heat lightning cracked the sky.
At night we lay in bed naked
as frogs fucked loudly at the pond
and bats made a bloody killing.
To my knowledge she
never tried to poison me
though the food she cooked often
tasted salty and left my throat
dry, my tongue licking
the white scum from my lips,
a hole burning in my gut.
When I'd start to make love to her
she curled up into fetal position
and wouldn't budge.
"Don't you want to make love?" I asked.
Her ass smiled at me
as if ready for anything, but the eyes
in the back of her head took aim,
waiting to pull the trigger if necessary.
"I do," she replied, curling up
into a tighter knot, "but not now."
Mosquitoes buzzing at the screen,
I waited for her hand to graze my thigh

or a breeze to come or a twister
to spin over the streets
and lift our bed high into the clouds
and let us fall toward earth
like seven-year locusts
climaxing in midair before they bury
themselves in mud.

NOTES FROM A LOVE LIFE

I once made love
to a thousand women—
it was a wild month,
and I still owed my father rent.
I sowed my seed
night and day, begetting
Adam, Eva, Rachel, Muffy
Terence, Alcibiades, Bunny,
Midge, Rona, Sasquatch,
Cordell Dewberry, Candy Berger,
Michelle, Janey—in other words,
the whole state of Missouri,
including the boot heel.
And I invented the phrase
"I don't believe it," which later
became "Show me,"
because of all the little bastards
in the Ozarks demanding cash
and claiming to be the son
of the son of God.
So what if I fell asleep after
or called Ginny Jesse
or Sarah Sally? So what
if I had many live-ins
but no wives? And so what
if after, I treated all my lovers
like sisters, and all my sisters
were lovers?
Once I brought a woman
to four thousand three hundred
and sixty-two orgasms, which
shattered all previous records.
I marked each orgasm on the wall
with colored chalk. By the time
our lovemaking was over,
the room resembled the cave
in Lascaux, filled with paintings
of bulls goring their gourds

and priapic cave dwellers
saluting the red asses of their lovers.
She floated away on a river
of pleasure or so I thought.
Only later did I learn,
she didn't like the way I kiss,
the taste of my skin,
or how my face contorts
with each triumphant thrust—
and not all orgasms are good.

WALKING UPHILL: A MEMOIR

Approaching the slope, Dram Beatty remembers
getting so drunk with James Dickey in Cambridge
they fell off a platform reading their poems,
caught and hoisted in air by the crowd,
stomping and yelling for more. "Dickey was an animal."
He stops to catch his breath halfway up,
his cheeks red and puffy, sweat festooned under his lush
        silver hair
as he stares out at the green valley and the federal-style
        white houses—
"I almost became an architect." And then there were his days
in rural Mississippi in 1964, mobilizing blacks,
leading them toward Civil Rights, "Talk about dangerous . . ."
Behind us the cows spit up grass, oblivious to history.
Now he tells me about photos he's taken of covered bridges
and old barns and men working on buildings and roads,
photos praised by Robert Frank and Walker Evans.
"I almost became a photographer," he says.
"Let's keep walking," I answer;
but he's taking deep breaths recalling his travels through Italy
with the minister of culture's beautiful assistant,
how they made love in the bathroom of the library before
        his reading.
Once he wrestled with Pablo Neruda
on a mountain in Chile while Robert Lowell
lay in his own vomit, reciting the odes of Horace
without missing a beat. While he puts his hands
on his knees, I look for a scarlet tanager or a blue kingfisher,
but nothing moves in the trees except the leaves.
In the gravel a robin puffs out his brown breast,
spitting and cursing, remembering the days
when he took some sparrow in the gravel,
and in the wind, her loose feathers flew off.

PRICE OF A KISS

Once I stole a necklace
from my mother's jewelry box
and gave it to Jackie Schreiber for a kiss.
The pearls hung like raindrops on stems.
"Close your eyes," she said,
as I leaned against a sycamore.

On the lawn a cardinal whistled at a dove
and two jays squawked on branches.
"Close your eyes," she said
and disappeared into broken violets,
into closed venetian blinds.
My cheeks burned as though wind-chapped.
A car blasted down the street
blowing dark smoke.

Once I stole a necklace from my mother
and white butterflies streamed
from moons hidden in cedar bushes.
Grasshoppers fell at my feet.
Clumps of seeds rode into the light.
At the door she held the necklace
in her hands, tears on her eyelashes,
punishing me with silence.

My father hit me.
I fell backwards onto the carpet,
sorry I had stolen from my mother,
sorry I had received only a tiny kiss,
staring at the pearls festooned in air
between my mother's thumbs,
and wondering what I might get
for a diamond.

THE TRUCE

We call a truce and agree to meet
at the café of slackers where flies
doze on tabletops
and wet rags hang from the ceiling
and even the music is too lazy to change.
You wear beads and an ensemble of correction.
I wear spikes and my best armor.
"It's silly to keep this going," you say.
Pigeons strut down the aisles
and the newspapers settle on the stools.
Ignoring me, you sharpen your pink nails.
I play with my nunchucks.
The juicer whips up a Mango Tango
which I slurp through a straw.
You sip your caffè latte.
The blenders grind on.
Coins clamor for a hearing.
At the cash register Polly asks everyone to listen,
someone's car is in danger.
We lean together as though gossiping
or revealing our secrets
but friendship is not possible
and the word "negotiation"
circles the room. We lay out
a map. You circle
my kingdom, I mark yours.
The truce is over.

UGLINESS

My sister was so ugly
our mother left her at the lake
with a family of ducks
and a basket of bread crumbs,
a cheap dowry. Pure ugliness
is just as rare as pure beauty
and should be highly valued.
Ask Ruth Wallerstein, whose son
resembled a fire hydrant
and always played the hunchback
in the yearly school production
of *The Hunchback of Notre Dame*.
"A gifted actor," Miss Frenzel commented
after every performance.
Whoever said beauty is in the eye of the beholder
was either looking in a mirror
or at an ugly child. My sister
floated there preening her feathers
until the ducks complained to the authorities
and my mother brought her home
in the car, my sister's wings
a little damp, but none the worse for wear.
"Maybe if we dyed her hair black,
instead of blond," my mother suggested,
"and let her bangs grow out,
she'd be easier on the eye."
"There must be a way to make
a buck off this," My father insisted.
My sister cried silently,
which was scary. Who would love her
with black hair? "Don't worry," I told her,
"one day we'll both fly away."
For two years she dated
a rotary telephone
named Todd, holding him
in her lap, bending down
to whisper in his ear, and waiting,
waiting for him to whisper back,

"I love you . . . I love you . . ."
At school, boys would not look her in the face.
On the street drivers catching
a glimpse crashed into cars or lampposts.
But squirrels kissed her hands
and wrens perched on her shoulders
lifting their lovely tails to the sky.

THE WAR ON FAT, FRONTENAC PLAZA

At 90, my mother wobbles
on the cobbled walkway. "Look
at that one," she declares.
She leans on me as she stares
at the heavy woman in a pink sundress
plodding toward us with a candy
bar and caramel corn.
"And she's got food in both hands."

I urge my mother forward,
though she's frail. "Mom, not so loud,"
I answer, but she fixes on the family
breaking into a large red box
of Mrs. Fields' cookies.
"No wonder they're all fat."

Is this the woman
who told her friend Ethel
to stop harassing her son
about being gay and be happy
someone else in this world loves him?

Fifty pounds overweight,
my father filled his plate
with brisket and potatoes while my mother
warned him not to get any fatter.
"What've you got against fat people?" he snapped.

For twenty years
she's lived on cottage cheese,
fatty corned beef
and chocolate chip poundcake
and she's still thin.

Sun pours through the glass wall.
Red and blue lights tint
the water spouting from the fountain.

She points at a man
squeezed into a metal deck chair,
"That one's eating two scoops
when he should be the one walking."

As we pass Sylvia's Pet Shop,
the parrots perk up, waving
their black beaks and mocking us
in the window. Multicolored
balloons sail toward the rafters:
"It wouldn't hurt you to take off
a few pounds either," she says.
"Look at that one," I answer.

Rebekah

Under the trees
a crow kills a crow
and Isaac cries for justice,
remembering the knife and the shadow,
the look in his father's eyes.

My sons come home—Esau,
wild and ravenous, devouring
bowls of stew,
Jacob laying his head
on a pillow of stone, dreaming
that angels wheel above him
like birds circling their prey.

Our tents vanish. The windows
shake, and silvery tubular
bells chime, but the camels,
their packs still full,
roam the naked desert,
and wings of moths beat
against my cheeks.

At the well,
I fill my jars with water
and let my long hair fall,
and the servant opens his bag
of gold bangles, and bitter bees
toss into the bright air.

I strike a deal with shadows,
the king of salt, his covenant
a burst of white in the wind.

Two

Cashing In

After he takes out his silver clip
of twenty sawbucks and tosses it on the table,
my father snoozes on the couch,
dreams made of Scotch.

My mother slaps the iron with her palm
to hear it hiss, presses
his white shirts. "He's tired,"
she says, "leave him be."

Then she sips black coffee
as she watches the stove,
the soup boiling on the burner,
lid shaking and shimmying.

I put my hand on my father's forehead,
the dark clouds of stubble
and sweat under his eyelids
like the smell of wet leaves.

Acorns drop on his new Buick.
Automatic car windows
go up and down.
Sycamores open their leaves.

I step inside my father's dream
and listen: "We'll be so rich
we'll live in a hotel.
We'll be so rich . . ."

THE BINDING

Lying down on an altar
of brambles, I closed my eyes
so I wouldn't be blinded and waited
for the worst to happen. My father

placed sticks on my chest
and said a prayer I'd never
heard before. At the corner
of my eyelids, the shadows deepened.

He took a deep breath,
then a powerful gust of wind came
between us, scattering the sticks
on the ground. I let my hand

brush my nostrils and caught
the scent of cedar and oranges.
The heavens creaked louder
while the detritus of our tribe flaked from my skin,

and alphabets of dust swirled
in the wind. In the murderous dusk
my father sat on a rock,
a sad procrastinator,

and drew pictures in the dirt
with his knife. I shook
my head—a nest of fire
in the red shower of the sun.

SUNDAY AT THE DELI

At the door a cold front meets
a warm front, snow and wind
coming in. Dishes clatter.
The order bell rings and rings.
In the center of the deli, where the air smells
of tzitzel bread, eggs, onions, corned beef, salty lox,
Uncle Izzy, a tailor, dabs his mouth
delicately, leans into the table: "I heard
Sid Wallerstein made a killing in the market."
"He's a crook," my fathers answers,
blowing steam off black coffee.

Over by the john door, Uncle Eddie—
a million bucks buried in his backyard—
places bets on the pay phone.
Izzy takes out a roll of quarters,
places it on the shiny Formica.
"Who isn't a crook these days?" he adds.
For a moment, my father and Izzy
remain silent, mulling over the mysteries of money,
the fortunes they'll never earn or steal.

When Eddie comes back to the table,
he brings Rosie, who leans over us with her order pad.
"Does the #5 come with juice?" Izzy asks.
"What do you think?" Rosie replies.
Snow reddens in the window, swirling.
Clouds camouflage the sun.

I pour salt into my palms,
close my eyes and say a prayer
over the clatter of the dishes. I ask
God for a winning card.
"What is this kid, a rabbi?" Eddie asks.
"Cut it out, Junior," my father commands,
raising his hand as I open my eyes
and blow my wish into the light,
and a desert falls at my feet.

BREAKING PITCH

My father raises his hand to signal "enough,"
but I'm still pitching, and the ball spins
off my fingertips—a breaking pitch
with so much stuff on it my imaginary batter
is too baffled to swing, so much stuff
the angels whistle, the crows near
the garbage cans take off in a flurry
of caws, and the mosquitoes burst in midair,
so much stuff my father, fear
in his eyes, hits the pavement,
behind him glass shattering.

Above the garage, Mrs. Golub, who runs
a vacuum cleaner over her wood floors every two hours,
yells out the window, "I told you something
bad would happen if you let that kid play here."
And Miss Lamar pushes her long
nose into the screen, "See if my car
has any glass on it," and Mr. Gorelick,
who sells silk ties to posh men's shops,
shouts, "Clean up the mess, boy."

I hear the cars on Clayton Road,
their tinny horns, the wind shaking
down leaves, the sound of the breaking
pitch trembling the wires that cross
from neighborhood to neighborhood, echoing
in shells strung from my best friend's
doorway, the white horsehide glinting
in the sun, a flash of light,
a prophecy of greatness.

Shaking his head, my father comes toward me,
his tightened fists warning me that I'll be sorry.
"Helluva curve," he mutters, "helluva curve."

FATHER TO SON

Junior, it's time to quit
perusing the penumbra, like a lost
moose licking the salt
at the side of the road. It's time
to quit the rainbow and all
the little doves that whisper
their intricate plots in your ear.
Blossoms rain on the lawn.
The bus stops at the corner
three times a day,
unloading a cargo of Abishags
in bright schmattes. Gather
your acorns while you can, Junior.
Get out of your funk. Let
the stink rise to the heavens.
The wind carries my meaning.
Get out and earn your fortune.
Rattle a few cages
and money will fly. Shake
the tree and the coins will fall
into your cup. Believe it
and the world is yours—
ten bucks a tuchis.

SON OF APOLLO

At the bar, my father pounds booze with buyers,
boasting about his new line of sportswear
that flies off the hangers at Marshall Fields.

They toast him: "Here's to your health
and wealth," then go to dinner, bowing
to plates of steak and prime rib, bloody.

Later he drives through the suburbs
like some kind of woozy king, running
lights and swearing at the fat, white moon.

He floors the gas pedal
and watches smoke rise in the rear view
and smells hot rubber on tar.

He breaks the sound barrier.
Sonic booms shake the houses
loose from hills.

The sun ignites trees.
His car rips a hole in space,
burning up the world.

ISHMAEL

I forgive your complicity, Father,
a nation lifting like
a white sheet, the tongue
uttering its twelve lost syllables.

I forgive your neglect,
my mother praying to the mist
that burned our faces—
your love like a split atom,

like a missile tearing off a limb,
like a blast that melts the skin,
leaving only a silhouette,

like a wasted body, like death
in the eyes of a hawk
drifting above a dry well.

Cities fall. Oil
oozes from the earth—your love
like a starving voice.
Armies of flies swarm flesh.

I aim my bow.
You won't live
to tell this story.

My Shammai

My Shammai curses when I stutter through my Haftorah.
"You call that Hebrew," he says and walks to the back of the
      synagogue,
"Recite again." My Shammai mocks me when I
      mispronounce "Leah."
"You say it like the goyim." He commands me to lie on the roof
and stare through the skylight. "What do you see?"
"Rabbi Fishman and Rabbi Nodel discussing Torah."
"You see nothing," he replies. My Shammai glowers
like a star, his death a flame for eternity.
He shakes in the wind, his hands trembling
with the disease he calls "fear of God."
Dust clings to his hair. He buys me
a new shirt and tie. "Comb your hair," he commands.
My Shammai is filled with truth like an éclair
bloated with custard. He prophesies
the fall of empires. He corrects me
as though I were a dog on a leash, but there is no treat.
My Shammai opens another carton of milk and blesses it.
My Shammai gives up a thousand lives as he paces behind
      my book.
He won't ever say "yes." "Because nothing is perfect."
He believes the end is coming
and soon after, the void to end all voids.
My Shammai cracks three eggs on the bowl and scrambles
      the yolks
and curses Earth for all she has taken.
He praises truth because it is without hope.
My Shammai stares into the mirror like a lost patriarch,
flinches at his own wizened face.
He rails and rails, but I can only listen
and help him back to his chair.

No One Called

No one called today with bad news.
No one broke down on the phone, describing
how he or she went just like that
with the blink of an eye. No one told me

to take the next plane and get a cab
from the airport. No one wanted me
to tell a funny story or share a memory.
No one expected me to clean out the rooms

and sort through the boxes, setting
aside a box of keepsakes for myself. No one
wanted me to remember how he loved to tell
a joke, how she always listened and laughed.

And no one called my name, waiting for me
as I crouched by the rocks and scattered
the ashes, stirring the river with a stick
until the current caught them.

THREE

COMICE

While sea creatures quivered
in a whale of a wave, while a vein
throbbed like a cursed tribe,
a knuckle hardening in the gut,
while nipples glinted in mirrors
and a moan vibrated over knotted strings,
I licked a Comice until
its russet coat melted,
and sweet juice welled up on my tongue.
I licked red grapes, bright seeds,
rocks, salty savannah grasses,
the velvet inside a pocket.
An orange moon teetered
on a pink trail. Striped
lemurs jumped into the light,
climbing higher and higher
into deaf branches. The spotted
leopard waited in the cattails,
his eyes bright with prey.
I licked gritty stones,
pearly caves,
milk seeping from pods,
spicy sauces from the fingertips
of the Nile. Invaders rode
rough waters behind polished wooden prows
shaped like the heads of horses.
The snake inside coiled and coiled.
I licked the wings of a bird
until nothing was left but feathers,
orange moon dropping into a ditch
as the silk robe struck the floorboard
and cried, "More, more . . ."
as Amaretta filled her luscious
frock, as a tuft of hair
floated toward the window, as the dewy
eye blinked and a little brown
sparrow told another lie.

THE ORGASM IN LATE AFTERNOON

after Nin Andrews

The orgasm was there, inside. I knew it
and she knew I knew it. I knocked
but she wouldn't come to the door. I called
her phone, ringing into voice mail.
I peeked in the window and saw her feet,
her bare legs rising into fleshy thighs.

"She's irritable, dyspeptic," the crow
in the driveway warned in a loud voice.
"Better let her have her way."
"I always give in," I answered.
"Don't listen to him," the robin, perched
on the branch of a birch, interjected. "He's bitter."

She was a queen bee, I could feel her power
humming in the cells of her house. But my jaw
ached, and my tongue was numb.
I felt dizzy from the smell of pollen
and nectar. My allergies had kicked in
and my whole face swelled.

"Take a rest," the robin said."
"Quit now," the crow countered, "are you nuts?"
The sun receded behind the hemlocks,
and a breeze cooled the sweat on my neck.
I whispered names into the window,
"honey, sweetie, sugar pie . . . open the gates,"

and still nothing happened.
Then I grabbed the knocker
and banged on her door for all I was worth.
She opened the upstairs window.
"Go home," she said, looking down at me,
"it's almost dinner time, and I need a nap."

I leapt up as though I could reach her
and yelled, "I want you to be happy—
I won't take no for an answer."

WALKING WITH CHUCK

At a white country church
where Methodists sell baked goods
to raise money for the fall
Monkey Dance, Chuck recalls
how he left his family
for another woman. "She touched me
in places I didn't know I had."
Earlier today,
Chuck took his maul
to three cords of wood.

Earlier today, he slaughtered
a pig and stuffed a hundred
sausages into casings. Earlier
he midwived a calf
after translating a tale
of two biblical scholars
punished for their lust. Hidden
behind a tree, they spied
on Susannah, which means lily,
as she bathed in the garden.

I pick up the pace, trying not
to listen. "She hovered over me
like a wreath of bees. She was crazy."
Then he bumps me, and I fall into
clover, gravel, clusters
of poison ivy. Now he praises
his ancestral home, his wife
perched like a canary, singing like a
finch, cooking exotic
dishes spiced with cayenne,
bay leaves and fenugreek.

"Give me a little space,"
I retort and brush myself off,
already itching, but he's walked far ahead.
Cars swerve around me, honking.
At the pond, a blue heron
stands on one foot, poised
to trap a meal. Red-winged blackbirds
reel in raucous debate.

Chuck says something pithy
to a big oak. In a field
some black-and-white-striped Susanna
chews up a mouthful of grass,
shakes her head forcefully to rid
herself of the rabbis whispering
sweet nothings in her ears.

Sunday Morning Breakfast

Elbows on the table, my uncle Harold
swears at his boss in Hungarian
for assigning him department stores
in small towns "where there is no money."
My aunt Ruth shakes her red hair,
"Harold, drink your juice."

From across the table,
my father looks down at me
as I take a bagel. "Wait for your mother,"
he commands, but he's already
eaten half his bagel and he's still chewing.

My mother never stops serving,
carrying in plates of scrambled eggs,
toasted bagels, onions, cream cheese,
canned peach halves, fruit cocktail, pads of butter,
tomatoes, jelly, pitchers of
water and juice, the coffee percolator.

Next to me, my sister rakes her eggs
into patterns on the plate,
while my cousin Nancy
puts a whole block of cream cheese
on her bagel.

My father looks at her in disbelief,
and Uncle Harold swears in Hungarian
but my mother rushes in,
stripping off the silver foil
from a new cream cheese,
offering it to my father and uncle,
"And there's another one in the fridge."

Before Nancy can lift her bagel
and cream cheese to her lips,
Harold pushes out his palm
as if signaling cars to stop at an intersection.
This time, he shouts in English,
"You can't eat all that."
I nod at her. As she bites in,
white bubbles float over the table,
rising toward the chandelier
until I reach up and pop them
with my fork.

ROUTE 12

On Route 12, I stopped for a lonely knish,
fell into the soup with a matzo ball.
On Route 12, I found a lily in the garden—
what a punim she had—bathing in cool scented water.
The elders hid behind the cedars reciting Talmud
and watching drops of water slide down
her breasts. On Route 12, I followed the river of chicanery
into the pearly purlieus where the rabbi robbed the ark,
then took off in a limo. On Route 12, the cantor kvelled
when his camel sung Kol Nidre, and the flies broke the fast,
swarming the honey cakes and figs.
On Route 12, a pretty slice of smoked salmon
lay on a bagel with an onion, and Moses swore at his herring.
The cracked synagogue floated on the horizon,
tribes clashing in lacy pink scrolls.

Left Hand

Happy to operate on his own,
the left hand wants a life of ease and prosperity,
though his knuckles whiten with tension
and often crack. Parrots arrive
at his fingertips. Black keys
snap back at him. With a sweaty palm
he loops his tie into a bulky double Windsor,
then discards the tie. He sells condos
floating on silt to alpacas
who can't resist a good deal.
He sells feathers to old pigeons
at outrageous prices, but pulls strings
for family and friends.
He wrings the neck of a towel
until it bleeds blue. He shakes
and shakes—still a few drops left.
He grips a sea monster so hard
her arm breaks off. He pounds
the head of an angel like a nail
until the angel offers him a map
of the promised land and goes back
where he came from with a concussion.
But you can't trick the left hand
because he knows all the tricks.
He holds on to twenty-dollar bills
with his teeth. He strikes a deal
with camels to deliver cargoes of salt.
He's a realist though some claim he's a cynic.
He carries a handkerchief for those
who will cry because of him.
He doesn't believe in regret
and never writes a sympathy card.
He cups a small bird in his hand
and says, "To hell with the Bushes."
He remembers his life on the Nile,
lifting huge stones into pyramids.
He remembers dinosaurs walking
over the savannah. He remembers

that he was once a pincer and then a claw
gripping clods of dirt.
At all costs he avoids his brother,
who holds the scepter of moral indignation,
who rises in anger and hate,
at a moment's notice, ready to kill.

SHALLOT

I get little bits of you all over me
while I bloody my index finger
trying to chop correctly and precisely,
like Jacques Pépin with his wide grin,
trying to ignore the dog banging
the glass door with her paw
and barking to get in
and the crows ganging up
on the sharp-shinned hawk.
I'm ready for an eclipse
that brings me salty waves, pelagic
pleasures. I'm ready to dance among
lemon wedges while the rosemary reaches
for the sun, and the orchid sways
and dips and red ladies drop
their skirts to their knees, wiggling free.
A rich, fat man gets stuck in the needle
eye of heaven, cumulus clouds
closing around him. A camel
clogs the drain. The sanguine sister,
sitting on her stalk, casts her net,
but nothing catches.
In the uncut grass crickets
rub their sticky legs,
calling the names of lovers.
Now you wait for me,
shimmying in a sleek pan—
your streaked layers translucent
in the glissando of sizzle—
giving up your bitterness
to the peppery oil.

Night of the Gnat

Just as we sat down to dinner with our guests,
the doorbell rang, and without waiting
for an answer, Ruth, the Jewish yoga guru,
danced through the unlocked door in a silk shawl.
"My gift to you," she said and placed
a shriveled lotus petal in Colleen's hands.

"It's a shame," I responded,
"we only have enough food for the four of us,"
but she had already grabbed a plate
and started helping herself to hefty servings
of Indian chickpea stew, broccoli,
and sautéed spinach with toasted walnuts.
"Bring me a bowl of the zucchini soup," she commanded.
Over my dead body, I thought and remained seated.

"In India, portions are very small."
She shook her head, perhaps remembering
the gnats and flies on the river Ganges.
Then she droned a blessing in Hindi for almost five minutes.
"What does it mean," Colleen asked.
"It's a prayer for goodness," Ruth answered.
She again told us about her teacher, Guru Beani,
a man of high holiness who has thousands of followers
and delights in gifts of jewelry.

When the yawning grew to a pitch,
Ruth pulled out finger cymbals, pinging them,
and intoned the story of her nights on the river,
how she let out her long wavy hair like the other Indian women,
praising the holiness of insects and all other creatures
whose karma have led them to this life,
how she sat in lotus position for twelve hours
and stared at the flame of the candle until it swelled into the sun,
gnats and flies settling on her lips and forehead—
but she never twitched or blinked.

When she requested another helping of chickpea stew,
one of the gnats that traveled with her from India
awoke and flew down her throat.
"Aren't you a vegan?" I asked.

First she gave out a feeble cough
then hawked up some phlegm and coughed some more,
her face turning red, her hands fanning the air
to signal she was choking.
"Give me Heimlich," she pleaded,
and stripped off her shawl and her long-sleeve shirt.

Miraculously, before we could move to rescue her,
she regained her breath,
and launched into one of Guru Beani's
parables about vanity
as I watched the moon rise from her lips
waiting for a revelation
or the gnat to fly back into the light.

Luna Moth

I thought it was a bat, looking for trouble,
but it was only a luna moth clutching the screen.
When it settled on my pillow, closing its wings,

I left the room and waited for it to fly out
but it remained in the cavity of my pillow
until I slipped a piece of cardboard

under the speckled body.
Then in anger it flew wildly through the rooms of our house,
a blessing gone awry, and before I could swat it

it vanished into some crack or
hidden place. Then I lay down again
and waited for you to open your eyes

but you gripped the sheets and held fast to sleep,
and the luna moth scudded through our bedroom, reading
my horoscope on the dust of the blinds.

IN MY BOOK

In my book you're a hot little terrier
with a sexy back end,
flicking the flies from your tail,
and I'm a mixed breed with brown eyes,
sharp nails and black whiskers much too
long for my muzzle, curling like a cat's.
I know a few tricks: Touch my fur,
rub my belly, lick my ears.
I roll in damp grass, I open my legs—
do it again—again.

On Behalf of the Prick

The prick wags his tail
when he's happy or hungry.
Can you blame him?
He can recite a single poem
in seven languages,
which should tell you something
about his devotion
to a single principle,
and which should make you
love him for his tenderness.
The prick's lips sparkle
with a special lip gloss.
His nature's bittersweetness,
sweet if you touch him,
bitter if you don't.
He's written a bible of sorts,
spreading the word
when he gets a chance.
When torpid,
he's not tumid, which is lucky
for you . . . nor, push comes to shove,
does he explode
with turgid force, except
perhaps if he smells turmeric
or remembers his tupelo roots.
Consider his cousin, the pygmy
chimp, a natural born cheater,
swinging from bash to bash.
Consider the long-tailed widow
bird, lounging around all day
with his angry harem. All in all,
you've got a good deal.
When necessary, he cleans house.
He even puts away the dishes
and the Tupperware while
you lie on your pillow. Evolution's
left him a little breathless.
So what if the walls are stained

and the mirror smeared
and you're slightly, or even totally, bemused.
Three minutes—he gets the job done.
Kudos to the prick.

Making It

"If you know what's good for you,"
my Uncle Jack rasped
chewing a fat green cigar
outside the Helpee Selpee Laundromat,
"you'll stay away from the shiksas."
I nodded, but the gray male pigeons
clustered on the high curb
flew off to chase trios of nurses
sashaying down Laclede
with their shopping bags.

Then he walked inside to empty
quarters from coin boxes
and clean lint from dryers,
and I broke down cardboard boxes
in the back room of the 4904 shop,
where my Aunt Evelyn cranked
the arm of the adding machine,
totaling the losses for the week.
"Why you run with the goyim?" she asked.
I shrugged as if to say, "God only knows."

At home, my mother sliced
the skin and meat from chicken bones,
then roasted the bones.
"Watch your smart mouth," she warned,
before I said anything,
and lifted the butcher knife
like Abraham on Mount Moriah.

On the steps every evening,
my sister mooned over
the black sidelocks of her fiancé,
an orthodox Jewish boy, until he
dumped her because his father shouted at him,
"She's not Jewish enough to boil an egg
without making it treif."

The wailing went on for weeks,
but her handsome Hassid never called again.
My father took me aside,
putting two fingers up to his lips
in our house of mourning,
"You want to get ahead with the goyim,"
he whispered, "you gotta learn
to play a little golf."

AT BURDICK'S

When Bud expostulates for me the real problem,
pressing his elbows into the tablecloth,
picking up a little butter grease,
I answer, "What's the problem?"

The waitress hovers a few feet away, ready to
take our orders, but afraid to break in.
He swipes his knife across the butter plate,
lifting two pats of butter before I can budge, and finishes

most of the bread in a few good bites.
A silver spigot spews foam into latte,
spoons tap porcelain cups and then
he again recounts his love affair

with the Russian specialist, who exposes
her inner lips to him on the floor of his office
every Tuesday and Thursday
and in the throes of orgasm screams, "Bravo, Karamazov!"

I yawn and yawn and soon
the waitress yawns and the young woman
bouncing a baby on her knee over hot chocolate yawns—
and the cashier yawns so loudly

the chandelier creaks back and forth,
and the bartender, polishing silver, glares at her
for her noisy disapproval.
Eager flies arrive at our table,

asking too many questions.
The noon light falls through the window
turning Bud's fine head of hair silvery.
As he lifts his elbows, I snag

the last pat of butter with my knife, smearing it
on my wedge of baguette, and
he waves his arms to signal
the waitress to come back.

Bud orders an omelet with crispy fries—
fifteen bucks—and I get a garden salad
for five bucks, thinking I'll fill up
on bread and mooch a few fries from his plate.

A little wine and he falls into a stupor
mumbling about his dinner with Tolstoy
in the little Vermont village town, Chicken Kiev.
"Leo's a Jew," I say, "and so was Levin."

And at that moment, Anna G enters the café
with a big fur muff. In the corner, cream
drips from Tsipkin's thick beard,
and Dostoyevski sips black tea over the Book Review

while flies clamor around our heads.
"The prince is an idiot," I say, "that's the real problem."

Yom Kippur

The chrysanthemums wag their heads, admonishing
me not to break the fast early for once,
not to give up on hunger. Don't I want
a clean slate? they ask—a congregation of optimists.
I close my eyes to atone for everything
I did that wasn't kosher. I beg
forgiveness for my comments
about Gloria's punim, for gazing too long
at Emily, blessed with naches,
for being such a schnorrer
my wife hides her purse from me,
for calling Russkie meshugana
when I know he's practicing circular
breathing, blowing out all the bad air
through his horn, letting go of his curses.
I open my eyes. A spider parachutes
over the dolls waving out the window.
The mums make me think I'm in Paris,
strolling down Place du Jour,
stopping in a café to share a croissant
and conversation with some perky poodle
pouting over espresso. A giraffe cadges
some change from a lonely tree.
Who says the world has to be cruel?
Who says the days are not bright here?
Chrome shines everywhere. The SUVs
hog two lanes. I ask for a better year.
Is anyone listening?
The mums sing Kol Nidre. They blow
the shofar. The rabbi bows his head.
He's always got one more thing to say.
Let's eat already.

FOUR

PRESIDENTIAL LOGIC

A little torture—water boarding,
starvation, sleep deprivation, electric
cattle prods on naked bodies,
if it pleases, the simple punch in the face—
can get us 7 code names
and 7 code names can get us
49 terrorist plots and 49 terrorist plots
can get us 100 extraordinary renditions, and a little more torture
can get us 1,000 cells connecting
all 7,777 cities with crowded avenues,
and 1,000 cells can plant
10,000 IEDs, which can blow away
the limbs of 50,000 civilians
and 50,000 civilians can cry for revenge
and give us the names of half a million
evildoers, and half a million evildoers
can lead us straight to the leaders,
hiding out in caves or small apartments,
and the leaders can give us the names
of all the passwords to secret accounts
and the secret accounts might lead
us to more leaders and then we can cut off
their supply of cash, and then a little more torture
can get us the names of 5 million more evildoers
and we can build a concrete prison
the size of a continent that will guard us
from the screams and cries,
and a continent of torture victims
can give us the names of all the dead
so we can dig them up
and find out what they know.

NOTE FROM THE EMPEROR

The emperor sends us a message—
"Avoid the streets
where work is done.
Stay in your homes."

Entire neighborhoods disappear.
The city is a mound of rubble.
The machines chew up metal and glass.
Bricks crack, boards snap.

At dusk, rain drizzles over bodies
piled on truck beds, glazes plows
and the long noses of tanks.
Still the cleansing continues.

"Forget what you've seen
and heard," he says;
"It didn't happen,
it didn't happen."

When the wailing stops,
widows curl into their sheets.
The fires die down.
A great tongue laps the rocks.

The emperor sends greetings
of peace and prosperity.
"Be happy you're alive," he says.
"Speak to no one."

But the air is full
of holes, and everywhere
we look,
someone is missing.

IRAQ

"The Way Forward . . ."

Today Abel had a question
for God.
Did he need to speak
for God to hear him?
He fell in the streets of Baghdad,
his body torn apart.
Today Cain lifted his head
in prayer. This time
God would accept his offering,
the smell of charred flesh
sweetening the air of heaven.
He raised his fist, declared
a victory for the fallen.

New Tape of Bin Laden

I should have ended on this—
the door closing, a last
note sounded, a shadow,

dust in the corner, the greasy
parrot singing my praises.
I should have let it go with a wisecrack,

a sardonic grin for you
to mull over while the room
shook and the chimes clanged

and the windows awoke to the grisly light,
voles running for cover,
while CNN played a new

tape of Bin Laden
and the President winked at the press,
announcing the success

rate of his war on evil. I should have
let go, salt to the wind,
mud in your eye . . .

MIRIAM AT THE WELL

God punished Miriam
with leprous spots.
Outside the walls of the city
she cursed her brothers
for their silence.
Frogs croaked.
Grasshoppers leaped
through air. Goats hid
from her. She covered
her face with a veil,
learning thirst, hunger,
staring into the eyes
of dead animals.
And then He called
her back, cured
her leprosy. She tapped
the timbrel and whispered
a song. She prophesied
from the wings of a crow,
the oil in her palm,
the bones of carcasses.
When she looked
into the well, she saw
light falling
on stones, on sharp
tongues, glittery
spall. She saw
the flame in water,
her ravaged
face, the well
gulping her thirst.

Bridge Street Café

We sat in the Bridge Street Café
where East meets West,
silent as always,
a dead fish on your plate
a dead fish on my plate.
Rain stitched the river.
A wild turkey stopped
traffic, sticking its long
neck into the white weeds.
The waiter, a goat
in a waistcoat, uncorked
a bottle of red and poured,
then backed away from us.
An old man with gout
snorted his snuff
and reclined in his ruffles.
Another year had gone by
like a tray of overpriced appetizers.
What did I remember?
We held hands once
under a big clock and kissed.
We strolled by the Black River
a day before it rose
over the banks and took out the bridge.
We studied a mock orange in the cemetery.
Your hair fell
over your shoulders.
Ducks lined up by the wading pool.
Someone was teeing off
from the green. Human bombs
went off in the streets.
The President declared peace.

Ararat

The dove never came back.
Everywhere we looked there were dead bodies,
piles of wood, shards of glass,
shreds of fabric, fragments of roofs,
jewelry glinting in sand.
As fish flew over us,
we lay gasping for breath,
our bodies speckled, grainy.

We gathered branches, started a fire,
said a prayer to the wave that drove
a wedge into our ark, the salt that startled our tongues.
Jackals ripped into corpses while birds
clustered around them, waiting for supper.
The world was shiny, dripping wet,
and once more wind blew into ash,
and the air smelled of charred flesh.

THE SURVIVORS

They come back with wool sweaters
and coats smelling of straw and shit

smoking their old cigars
ashes flaking from chin and cheeks.

They come back with glistening shells
pain in their joints—rooms of water.

Salt glittering on their lips
they walk on rock

where fish gasp and choke
and stars cluster in sand.

Sun rains into the abyss.
They come back with ruined hands and backs

hurling coins across oceans
building bridges with knots and fists

digging up cities of corpses
rotting under the rainbow

as doves fly out of their pockets
scavenging the carnage.

SOTTO VOCE

for Roy Nathanson

Call it luck—tonight you get
a seat on the subway
and don't have to hunch
with your saxophone case and backpack,
gripping the center pole.
The rabbi next to you raps about his new
Cadillac and his congregation
of ants. Dead yarmulkes bob
in the watery waves of the windows.
Call it luck—the Wall Street
mogul gives you a tip,
"Sell your wife and kid and rescue
a building in Red Hook.
Then you won't have to ride
the subway every day
or hear your students blast
their horns in your eardrums."
Walls crumble in front of you.
Joshua gets up and waves a sign,
"Free dinner at the league of Rosicrucians."
The rail sparks, but no fire. Pigeons
wait on the platform
gripping their briefcases
like bombs. Under the noise
a song ticks, as everyone stares
at their feet, as the newspapers
spread over the floor and the fuses glow,
sotto voce, sotto voce.

SALESMAN

In the middle of a sentence,
his black hair oozing oil,
his burgundy wingtips glinting—buyers
at department stores in Minneapolis
waiting for his grips to arrive,
for the curdled blouses, for the free drinks—
he got up to leave
and the fall air reddened
and leaves covered the bright yellow wings
of his Cadillac, fingers stroking a coarse music
from the teeth of a metal comb
as bills wadded in pockets
flew out like jays croaking at doves
and when the highway called for him,
when the hawk clamored, when a clapper gonged,
when a bloody fork lifted, when the sleek hood ripped,
he drew blood from the painted stripe,
from asphalt, gravel,
blood gushing from his crushed legs, his broken tongue,
and a cloud of locusts twisted over dried grass
hurling into the empty windshield—
in the middle of sentence a family of flies
filling his mouth . . .

LADDER

As I lay on a bed of sand, waiting
for sleep to find me, a splintery ladder
descended from heaven, but maybe it was a tree layered
with thick bark, its country of branches
bearing plump fruit. Wraiths flew up
and down while crows ripped worms from the earth
and vultures hovered over a pack
of jackals that found a mound of corpses,
and a billion glittering seeds fluted through the hollows.
I closed my eyes until nothing was left,
but a voice sweeping over bone.
In the morning, as my brother gathered his armies,
I raised the dust of ancestors—
plunged deeper and deeper into the desert.

Friday Night Service

As the rabbi cradles the scroll,
my aunt salutes his black limo
and my uncle Harold bows
to the Rabbi's elegant wool suit,
purchased at Klein's—50% off—
and my sister remembers his first wife,
"Too frail to even break bread."
Silk ties discounted to five bucks
dangle from double chins
and mouths and noses snort
in a deep slumber.

As the rabbi cradles the scroll,
wives weep over mahjong tiles
and husbands place bets
on the outcome of the war.
Snakes scour the Nile
for a handful of figs.
A chariot flares in hard
blue mirrors, Elijah
curling in a wreath of smoke.
An axe head bobs
on the surface of the water, tens and
twenties flying out of pockets.

As my mother strikes her palm,
"I wouldn't give a dime to that crook,"
wine spills from my lips
staining my new coat. Lacy
dresses float over honey cake.
Rubies dance through gold
doors. The palace on the hill
glitters, and Solomon's ark
smokes another army.

Bob Dylan Is God

Dylan is God. You want proof?
Look at his scruffy beard, tormented eyes,
scarred hands healed after centuries,
his stomach still a little bloated
from his time on the cross.

Look how the goyim
follow him everywhere.
Even birds copy his songs,
singing from sturdy branches.
His words raise snakes up from the dust.
Satan buys all his CDs
and plays them for friends.

God writes his own songs and prayers
so people won't misquote him.
Money and fame are vanities, he claims.
All night women bang against
his four-posted bed, looking for salvation.

He's a tiger, he's a lamb.
He writes, "Jesus strangled Moses
for a matzo. And me I scattered the hoses
and went into a wilderness of roses."

The rusted garden blooms again.
God disappears when you need him.
That's how God is. That's how Dylan is.
If you say the word God, Dylan answers.
Tickets to a concert cost more than
a Passover weekend with the Pharisees.

Once he came back as a duck,
quacking in Hebrew, davening
on High holidays, leading the children
out on the water. Once
he swallowed fire in a tent
and exhaled gold coins
and watched the audience tear itself apart.

Joan Baez says, God's a prick—
what does she know?
She's still singing his songs.

Eliot Was a Great Poet

T. S. Eliot was a great poet.
The wasteland wrote him a postcard,
scribbling praises on both sides.
Bob Dylan mentions him in a song.
He drank tea and pretended to be English.
He attended the Anglican Church,
letting his lips form somber amens.
Once he ate matzo ball soup
and thought he was Jewish.
He kept touching his nose,
which felt as though it were growing,
while Harvey Ginsberg tried
to sell him a box of perma-press shirts
and some silk-look ties. Jews
spoiled his appetite. After talking to one,
he often felt waves of nausea flush
his face and weaken his knees.
In the morning, while he ate his scone with jam,
a Jew squatted on the sill, singing
hallelujahs. At night bats
with Jew faces sneered at him
whistling through the rafters.
Secretly he craved gefilte fish,
chopped liver, lox with cream cheese,
a zaftig woman. But then
he would remember what old Ez said
about the Jew and money.
The Jew is the root of all evil.
Eliot cut a dashing figure
on the dance floor, fox-trotting
under the lights with a beautiful slip,
held lightly at waist and shoulder.
His shoes trampled over Jews.
He coughed up Jews in his phlegm
and squished them in his handkerchief.
Jews shone in the light.
Eliot's a great poet. Ask the new critics.
Ask the old critics.

So what if he lectured on strange gods
just after Hitler came to power.
So what if he thought Jews a blight on culture.
How can we know the dancer from the dance?
The life of the man or the life of the art?
Either-neither. Now he's ten
molecules on the tongue of a Jew,
a bubble of spit floating toward poetry heaven.

Rosh Hashanah

"This is a time for reflection,"
Rabbi Borax says in a mass email.
I hold my own service.
The moths clinging to the screens
pray to get in. The orchids open
their lovely legs. At the end
of the row, crows badger
each other over hymnals.
I cut the shofar loose.
My dog smells the blasts
and heads downstairs.
What kind of Jew am I?
The kind women at cash registers
glare at, the kind with scalloped
edges and frayed hair,
whose voice rises into prophetic zeal
over the slightest hint of a problem.
I smell tsimmes, brisket,
roasted potatoes, kugel.
I smell candles burning,
and apples dipped in honey
a thousand miles away.
No one in the community
invites me for dinner.
They probably don't even know
I know I'm Jewish.
I remember floods,
earthquakes, bombings,
diseases, deaths—
the misery in 2008.
Why would anyone argue
over their Jewishness?
I flick the lights to get God's
attention. I draw another glass
of wine from the box. I'm
my own shabbos goy,
carrying enough cash
to get in to a movie

and buy some popcorn.
This year will be another year
of war just like last year.
What should I pray for,
a little less blood,
another day on earth?
I bless my wife, my dog,
everyone I love
and everyone I don't love.
I do not bless the new year of kings.
I bless the new year of new years,
the act of creation.
Let's begin again.